Through Life's Window

Carl G. Carlozzi, D. Min.

THE CHURCH HYMNAL CORPORATION, NEW YORK

In Loving Memory of my Father
Carl M. Carlozzi, DDS

The Church Hymnal Corporation
800 Second Avenue
New York, N.Y. 10017
5   4   3   2   1

Contents

Preface

God made us free so that we might respond to him
openly and in a manner that is natural to us. He
requires of us no special words or liturgical format,
only an honest outpouring of the inner self. To pray is
to make this response to a God who has given and
continues to give of himself in and through all of life.
We are called simply to exercise our freedom by
opening our eyes and expanding our vision so that
we may behold the unfolding saga of his wondrous
presence through life's window.

"For I was an hungred, and ye gave me meat: I was thirsty, and ye gave me drink: I was a stranger, and ye took me in."

Matthew 25:35

Adoption

I've got to be honest, Lord.
Love someone else's child?
Never!
We discuss. . .
I say, "No!"
She says, "Yes!"
We argue.
And so it goes.

The years go by. . .
And somehow, in your love and her persistence,
I begin to change.
Lord, I don't understand myself.
I'm scared,
    excited,
    skeptical,
    hopeful.
And then, she arrives. . .
And I arrive at a new understanding of love.

Love someone else's child, Lord?
Always!
She is ours! ! !

"And he bearing his cross went forth into a place called the place of a skull, which is called in the Hebrew Golgotha: Where they crucified him, and two other with him, on either side one, and Jesus in the midst."

John 19:18,19

A Crucifix

Drooping low between unfurled arms,
The body hangs. . .
Rigid.
Hands and feet skewered by rivets of steel. . .
Unfeeling,
Unknowing,
Transfixed in impersonal mold.
Silent,
Quiet,
Still,
The sculptured Christ makes no gasps of despair,
                              no cries of anguish,
                              no shrieks of pain.
It is over.
The work is wrought.
The artist has gone home.
The contrived Christ hangs. . .
Impaled,
Alone.

The earth trembles. . .
The light grows dim. . .
The veil is rent asunder.
It is over.
The deed is done.
The executioner has gone home. . .
Mankind has gone home. . .home to forget.
The crucified Christ hangs. . .
Impaled,
Alone.

My son, I am still alone. . .
Alone in your brothers whom you have hammered on the cross. . .
The cross of your prejudice,
              apathy,
              hatred.
My son, how long must I hang. . .
Impaled,
Alone.

Will you not help me down?

"He was in the world, and the world was made by him, and the world knew him not. He came unto his own, and his own received him not."

John 1:10,11

Telephone

Lord, what a wondrous little box.
Ten digits and one thin wire. . .
Reaching most of humanity.
Potential unlimited,
But, yet, so restrictive. . .
Millions of wrong numbers.
Think of it, Lord,
Personal encounter the sole barrier between wrong and right. . .
And even that is no guarantee.
How frustrating it is. . .
Not even our relationship with you transcends this barrier.
Many don't know we share this common bond,
And if I should call,
They'd hang up.
And even most of us who are united in you,
Have no relationship with one another. . .
For if I should call and mention your name,
Chances are,
The receiver would also drop.
Lord, I guess you know this all too well,
For in calling us. . .
I-NCA-RNA-TION often received,
No answer.

"Wherefore they are no more twain, but one flesh. What therefore God hath joined together, let not man put asunder."

Matthew 19:6

Till Death Do Us Part?

Lord, here they sit. . . intimate enemies.
Love,
  Honor,
    Cherish,
All forgotten words on the battleground of life.
I want,
  I desire,
    I need,
      I demand,
Everything in egotistic reverse. . . asunder.
The one in Christ now two in themselves. . . fragmented,
                                              fractured,
                                              broken.
Lord, help them to transcend the resentment,
                              the bitterness,
                              the hurt,
                              the suspicion.
Take away their prejudice,
          their self-seeking,
          their fear of speaking the truth,
          their fear of hearing the truth.
Lord, bring them back to their beginning in you. . .
Where faithfulness and patience,
        wisdom and true godliness,
        respect and forbearance,
        trust and caring,
Made their home a haven of blessing and of peace.

"For wisdom is better than rubies; and all the things that may be desired are not to be compared to it."

Proverbs 8:11

Bookshelves

Jacketed into a multicolored rainbow,
Silently they stand. . .
    their voices hushed,
    their thoughts imprisoned,
    their potential restrained.
Stately lined in resolute posture,
Each awaits. . .
    Awaits the touch of curious hand,
        the light of searching mind,
        the warmth of human heart,
        the breath of exegetic life.
Lord, I pray. . .
    guide my hand,
    enlighten my mind,
    open my heart,
That I may behold the presence of your Living Word.

"For now we see through a glass, darkly; but then face to face: now I know in part; but then shall I know even as also I am known."

I Corinthians 13:12

Guided By The Spirit

Thy will be done!
I'm sure it will, Lord, but. . .
Who really knows what your will is?
I pray and get one answer.
My brother prays and gets another answer.
And, yes, Lord. . .
Still others pray and get even different answers.
We all claim your will. . .
And in our pious certainty we fight,
                              we bicker,
                              we denounce.
Just think of it, Lord. . .
We do all of this in your Name.
Your will?
Who knows?
All I know is this. . .
We do see through a glass darkly!

"Behold, how good and how pleasant it is for brethren to dwell together in unity!"

Psalm 133:1

A Typewriter

All before me. . . nothing yet devised.
Precisely splattered,
Responsive to the touch,
Uncommon keys awaiting a unifying strike!
qwertyuiop
asdfghjkl
zxcvbnm
Thoughts unformed,
Feelings unexpressed,
Words unspoken,
The treasury of human language yet unborn.

Lord, I look at the family of man. . .
Divided,
Independent creatures,
Spasmodically dotting earth's landscape. . .
A veritable compendium of egotistic designs.
What family?

Lord, strike the keys of our diverse hearts.
Make us responsive to your touch. . .
That our lives may come together,
Born anew in thee,
Instruments of unity.

"This is the day which the Lord hath made; we will rejoice and be glad in it."

Psalm 118:24

A New Look At Life

Thank you, Lord, for the blessings of this day. . .
    For the dawn and fresh breath of life,
    For the snow and invigorating air,
    For the donut and steaming coffee on my way,
    For the labor and creative challenge of opportunity.
But especially, Lord, thank you for the people. . .
    All kinds of people,
    Your people!
Thank you for enlivening my mind's eye to behold. . .
    Your presence as a light in the shining faces of children,
              as a flame in the warmth of clasped hands,
              as a tear in the eye of those who are troubled,
              as a voice in the fellowship of worship.
Thank you, Lord, for your presence in all.
Thank you, Lord, for all in your presence.

"Jesus said unto her, I am the resurrection, and the life: he that believeth in me, though he were dead, yet shall he live: And whosoever liveth and believeth in me shall never die. Believest thou this?"

John 11:25,26

Intensive Care

The respirator pulses out its steady beat. . .
One of your faithful, Lord, trembles,
                          throbs,
                          convulses.
So close to heaven and yet so far.
Such a good man, Lord. . . kind,
                          sensitive,
                          loving.
Why?
Why this agony,
          pain,
          torment?
Please, Lord, take him home!

The hours pass. . .
Family members cry,
Nurses scramble,
Physicians confer,
Another round of coffee. . . somehow bitter,
                          yet refreshing.
We wait. . . wait. . . wait. . .

Look up, my son,
The agony is over,
The new life begun!
Your friend and I now share eternity. . .
The heaven of loved ones reunited.
So be happy,
          trusting,
          confident,
          comforted.
I am the resurrection and the life!
And you, your friend, and all my faithful are now, as always. . .
A part of that life.

"And why beholdest thou the mote that is in thy brother's eye, but considereth not the beam that is in thine own eye?"

Matthew 7:3

She's Found The Lord

Born Again!
That's what she tells me.
Quoting scripture with machine gun velocity, but. . .
Invalidating every word through divisive manner,
                          self-righteous attitude,
                          unfeeling insensitivity.
Another hollow hypocrite out to save us all,
Blinded by the beam in her own eye.
So eager,
   pious,
      moralistic.
Twisting love into condemnation. . .
Hating sin and sinner alike.
Lord, save me from divine name-droppers,
Who in speaking your word. . .
Never hear it themselves.

"Therefore seeing we have this ministry, as we have received mercy, we faint not."

II Corinthians 4:1

Ordination

Earthly commission,
With divine imperative. . .
The awesome responsibility of serving others for Christ.
Called to be more than you are. . .
Giving the triumphs to Christ,
Heaping the failures upon yourself,
A constant tension borne out of joy,
                              despair,
                              excitement,
                              temptation,
                              fulfillment,
                              defeat.
But yet,
Once touched by the Hand of God. . .
You rejoice in a life of possible impossibilities.

"And the Word was made flesh, and dwelt among us, full of grace and truth."

John 1:14

Christmas

From eternity to here,
Human experience in reverse. . .
Messages from angels,
  Virgin birth,
    A Messiah without an army,
      A king in fear of a baby,
        Giving not receiving,
God proclaiming himself as man.

"Wherefore I abhor myself, and repent in dust
and ashes."

Job 42:6

Ash Wednesday

Ashes to ashes,
The reality of human existence sealed upon the flesh.
An eschatological symbol,
    warning,
    reminder.
Repentance. . .
The dust of degradation removed.
Absolution. . .
Eternal destiny assured.

"And a very great multitude spread their garments in the way; others cut down branches from the trees, and strawed them in the way."

Matthew 21:8

Palm Sunday

Triumphal entry. . .
Ignominious exit.
Hope to despair,
  Expectation to despondency,
    Anticipation to decimation,
Humility to be humiliated.

"And he sent Peter and John, saying, Go and prepare us the passover, that we may eat."

Luke 22:8

Maundy Thursday

The table is spread.
The common meal begins.
A sign is given, a foretaste of things to come. . .
He who offers, Himself to be offered.
Bread is broken. . .
    A body prepared.
Wine is poured. . .
    Blood awaits libation.
Unknowing,
Gathered disciples partake of what will become the feast of life.
Christ awaits consecration upon the altar of death.

"And it was the third hour, and they crucified him."

Mark 15:25

Good Friday

The hands which blessed. . .
    Pierced.
The eyes which illuminated. . .
    Closed.
The voice which taught. . .
    Silent.
The blood which redeemed. . .
    Spilled.
The heart which loved. . .
    Broken.
The life which offered. . .
    Gone.

It is finished!

"And very early in the morning the first day of the week, they came unto the sepulchre at the rising of the sun."

Mark 16:2

Easter Morn

He is risen!

All is new,
      transformed,
      resurrected.
The stone is rolled away. . .
    Creation bursts its prison,
     Life blossoms afresh with meaning,
      Mankind passes revitalized through the gates of death,
And I am made whole.

The Lord is risen indeed, Alleluia!

"And suddenly there came a sound from heaven as of a rushing mighty wind, and it filled all the house where they were sitting."

Acts 2:2

Pentecost

Enlightened with tongues of courageous fire,
Weak hearts and minds burst into flame. . .
A consuming fire soon to enkindle all of mankind.
The new age begins.
The Comforter has come.
The Lord dwells in his people and they in him.

Alleluia!

Come, Holy Ghost, our souls inspire,
And lighten with celestial fire!

"Lord, make me to know mine end, and the
measure of my days, what it is; that I may
know how frail I am."

Psalm 39:4

The End Is The Beginning

God, I don't want to die. . .
I'm afraid!
So much of life awaits to be lived. . . work unfinished,
                                    friends unknown,
                                    love unfulfilled.
Oh that I might see the dawn of another day,
                            another month,
                            another year.
It just isn't there, though, is it Lord?
How foolish I have been. . .
To take the wonderousness of life so lightly,
                            so complacently,
                            so ungratefully.
Oh Lord, I pray. . .
Fill these last moments with peace,
                        with thankfulness,
                        with joy.
Peace. . . that I may feel your eternal presence in these lonely
        and anxious hours,
Thankfulness. . . that I may be truly grateful for all past gifts
        of life and love,
Joy. . . that I may consider my heavenly home which awaits beyond
        this bond of affliction.
And so, Lord, let me know my end in certain confidence of your mercy.
Help me to trust in your love. . .
Your love which forgives the unforgivable,
                        brings light out of darkness,
                        and resurrects the dead to newness of life.

"Pure religion and undefiled before God and the Father is this, To visit the fatherless and widows in their affliction, and to keep himself unspotted from the world."

James 1:27

A Parish Call

The years have past.
The autumn of life draws to a close.
Family and friends are gone. . .
And isolated within walls of lonesome silence,
    A tired but faithful heart beats out its welcome.
Trembling hands reach to enfold a stranger's hands. . .
    And we are strangers no more.
Eyes cloud, reddening with tears of joy,
The joy of finding that someone does care.
The love of Christ wells up in our midst,
And we know, without speaking. . .
Christ is with us!

"Rejoice in the Lord alway: and again I say, Rejoice."

Philippians 4:4

Got A Minute, Lord?

What a great day, Lord!
Thanks for everything. . . my life, family, friends, food.
But, most of all Lord,
Thanks for being you.
Excuse me if I seem to ramble on. . .
But I'm happy,
       joyful,
        beaming.
I just can't help it Lord.
You've done it all. . .
And I just thought you ought to know.
So thanks again, Lord,
You're great!

"And the light shineth in darkness; and the darkness comprehended it not."

John 1:5

Lost Opportunities

INCARNATION. . .
   We didn't receive you.
REVELATION. . .
   We didn't perceive you.
CRUCIFIXION. . .
   We didn't love you.
RESURRECTION. . .
   We didn't believe you.
ASCENSION. . .
   We didn't want you.
REDEMPTION. . .
   We didn't appreciate you.

And we wonder why we are in Hell!

"Come, ye children, hearken unto me: I will teach you the fear of the Lord."

Psalm 34:11

Suffer The Little Children

Suffer is the word for it.
Surely, Lord, you can't be serious?
Why those little demons are enough to drive me mad.

When I'm serious, they're laughing. . .
    When I'm laughing, they're serious.
When I'm eager, they're tired. . .
    When I'm tired, they're eager.
When I'm conservative, they're radical. . .
    When I'm radical, they're conservative.
When I'm rude, they're polite. . .
    When I'm polite, they're rude.
When I'm happy, they're sad. . .
    When I'm sad, they're happy.
When I'm yelling, they're quite. . .
    When I'm quite, they're yelling.

Love them?
Lord, give me strength!
Ask me anything, Lord, but please. . .
Don't ask me to love a group of ten year olds!

"But he, willing to justify himself, said unto Jesus, And who is my neighbour?"

Luke 10:29

How Could You, Lord?

Look at him, Lord, if you can bear it. . .
    a decaying wreck of what was once a man,
    sprawled across that battered bench.
The stench of sweat and whiskey pervading every ounce of air,
His eyes closed in toxic stupor,
His face stubbly bristling and etched with lines of filth,
His hands cracked,
        twisted,
        stained.
His hair thin,
        yellow,
        dirty.
Surely, Lord, you couldn't have died for him.
Really, now, as if you could love him as you love me. . .
If you could love him at all?
How could you?
A repulsive wreck. . . offering nothing,
                giving nothing,
                only taking.
Hear me, my son. . .
Look at him!
Do you not see me?
Will you pass by my Cross and not see. . .
See my broken body stained with blood,
    my face twisted in anguish,
    my hands pierced with the nails of your callousness.
Will you pass by me again?
Will you offer nothing,
        give nothing,
When I have given you all.

"Labour not for the meat which perisheth, but for the meat which endureth unto everlasting life, which the Son of man shall give unto you: for him hath God the Father sealed."

John 6:27

The Lord's Table

Encouragement,
  Understanding,
    Compassion,
      Healing,
        Assurance,
          Reconciliation,
            Inspiration,
              Strength,
                Thankfulness,
The Living Presence of Christ made manifest.
Renewed,
Revitalized,
Made whole,
I can no longer live for myself alone.

"Wait on the Lord: be of good courage, and he shall strengthen thine heart: wait, I say, on the Lord."

Psalm 27:14

Solitude

Lord, I'm so alone tonight.
Surely, you know and feel my loneliness.
After all, you've said that you understand. . .
"Come unto me all ye that travail and are heavy laden."
That's what you said,
Isn't it?
Well, here I am!
Lord, I've tried. . .
But there's something missing,
Missing inside of me.
Sure I love you, Lord.
Your love wells up within me as a fountain.
Oh, if I could but share this love. . . share it with one I love.
I've waited. . .
Waited so long,
But she is nowhere in sight.
Where is she, Lord?
Is it really that much to ask?
I hope not. . .

Trust me, my son. . .
She is on her way,
On the way of your heart and of my love.
I know, for I am Love.
Wait for her as she waits for you. . .
Trust me, my son.
You shall come together in my kairos,
As I did come together with your brethren. . .
In the fulness of time.

"Ye blind guides, which strain at a gnat, and swallow a camel."

Matthew 23:24

A Manner Of Living

Mortgaged to the hilt. . .
    Pretending to wealth.
Condemning sinners. . .
    Forgetting one's own past.
Bold in opinion. . .
    For the sake of appearance.
Berating the poor. . .
    Having never experienced discrimination.
Quoting scripture so piously. . .
    Lusting in your heart.
Giving loudly to charity. . .
    Only to reduce tax liability.
Lauding the good life you have earned. . .
    When what you have has come through probate court.

Hypocrite!

"And the Lord God formed man of the dust of the ground, and breathed into his nostrils the breath of life; and man became a living soul."

Genesis 2:7

Earthly Irony

Just a pile of dirt. . . far from it!
Dirt is cheap and common, but yet. . .
   It cradles the foundation for all that is built in splendor.
Dirt contains germs and vermin, but yet. . .
   It is the source of organic nutrients and life-giving food.
Dirt makes us filthy, but yet. . .
   It produces the clean beauty of nature.
Dirt creates mountainous obstacles, but yet. . .
   It provides the challenge of adventure.
Dirt covers over the bodies of our dead, but yet. . .
   It reminds us of the Creator who brings the dead to life.
How ironic, Lord.
We even think of some of your people as dirt, but yet. . .
   On this important aspect of your creation,
   We seem to lose all our vision of inherent potential.

"To every thing there is a season, and a time to every purpose under heaven."

Ecclesiastes 3:1

A Moment In Time

Lord, it's a quarter to eight. . . a seemingly uneventful moment.
Or is it?
Somewhere, someone is. . .
Making love,
  Stealing,
    Laughing,
      Overdosing,
        Fighting,
          Being married,
            Playing tennis,
              Having a drink,
                Crashing in a car,
                  Sleeping,
                    Plotting murder,
                      Throwing up,
                  Committing adultery,
              Praying,
            Giving birth,
          Lying,
        Working,
      Filing for divorce,
    Dying,
    Swearing,
  Eating,
 Waging war,
And a thousand other things.

My son, consider. . .
At some moment in time,
Someone else's eventful moment may very well be yours!

"And, having made peace through the blood of his cross, by him to reconcile all things unto himself; by him, I say, whether they be things in earth, or things in heaven."

Colossians 1:20

A Symbol Of Hope

```
                    I
                    N
                    C
S   A   L   V   A   T   I   O   N
                    R
                    N
                    A
                    T
                    I
                    O
                    N
```

The Cross of Christ. . .
Life to death to life.
Your key, Lord,
To a redeemed creation.

"From whence come wars and fightings among you? Come they not hence, even of your lusts that war in your members?"

James 4:1

World Affairs

Big children with human toys,
Playing at life as a game.
Breathing pawns shifted,
                    manipulated,
                    sacrificed,
As if somehow nothing mattered. . .
Nothing but a new and more exciting strategy,
An esoteric battle of wits beyond all humanitarian concern.
Seduced by power,
  Intoxicated with self-serving flattery,
    Overblown through conceit,
So many immature and unfeeling egotists lay waste mankind.

"The ants are a people not strong, yet they prepare their meat in the summer."

Proverbs 30:25

The Big Apple

Madly rushing,
No one speaking. . .
Like so many ants,
Scrambling over the core of an apple.
But yet, Lord,
While the seeming confusion of ants,
Is an ordered attack for the common good. . .
We humans bump,
        shove,
           trample,
Each to satisfy himself,
    to protect what is his,
    to ignore the needs of others.
Strange, isn't it?
We are the ones who are really confused.

"Wherefore I say unto you, All manner of sin and blasphemy shall be forgiven unto men: but the blasphemy against the Holy Ghost shall not be forgiven unto men."

Matthew 12:31

Fire

Glowing embers of comfort to the flames of tragedy. . .
One source,
With the radical disparity of good and ill.
So much, Lord,
Like we your children. . .
Love to hate,
  Compassion to killing,
    Tenderness to terror,
      Understanding to condemnation.
So often, Lord. . .
We ignite the tongues of fire,
Into the blaze of hell.

"Nevertheless let every one of you in particular so love his wife as himself; and the wife see that she reverence her husband."

Ephesians 5:33

Let's Go See The Minister!

So you want to get married. . .
Why?
Because you want more sex,
                    security,
                    happiness,
                    attention,
                    companionship?
You can find that in a thousand other ways.
Don't come to me unless you're prepared. . .
Ready to take on sacrifice,
                    trust,
                    differences of opinion,
                    loyalty,
                    hardship,
                    living for someone other than yourself.
Remember, this is God's House, and here. . .
Marriage is a Sacrament,
Not a certificate of personal convenience.

"In my distress I cried unto the Lord, and he heard me."

Psalm 120:1

Surgery

Lord, tomorrow is the operation. . .
Christ, I'm scared!
Everyone says it's routine. . .
Well, good for them,
They're not the ones who are going to be knocked out,
                                        cut,
                                        biopsied,
                                        stitched.

So, if you're listening, Lord,
I could sure use a dose of peace of mind.
Damn it, Lord,
You better be listening!
I've prayed,
      pledged,
      worked for you. . .
Done just about everything over the years,
To keep that church of yours going.
So now it's your turn. . .
Just see to it Lord,
That I keep going.
If you think I'm asking for a miracle,
I am!
Why not?
You're in the miracle business, aren't you?

My son, I hear you!
What makes you think I would run out on you now?
I never have before.
So lay back,
Close your eyes,
And turn things over to me.
After all. . .
I know what I'm doing,
Even if you think no one else does.
So relax,
And let me take care of you.
That's what I'm here for!

"Thou shalt love thy neighbor as thyself."

Matthew 22:39

Furniture

So many uses. . .
I can sit on it,
      neglect it,
      stand on it,
      break it,
      eat on it,
      abuse it,
      sleep on it,
      discard it,
      play on it,
      put things on it.
Lord, how many times do I treat people like pieces of furniture. . .
To be used as an "it" for my own ends and desires.
Help me to remember, Lord,
That people should be appreciated,
              understood,
              assisted,
But most of all. . .
People should be loved.

"And ye shall know the truth, and the truth shall make you free."

John 8:32

Penance

Solemn confrontation. . .
A moment of truth,
Both painful and refreshing.
Christ sanctifying the present,
    reclaiming the past,
      giving hope for the future.
Another miracle of faith. . .
Holy Spirit impregnating human spirit.

"But Jesus said unto him, Follow me; and let the dead bury their dead."

Matthew 8:22

Calling Hours

Laid out in gross display. . .
An empty shell,
Attracting inane comments,
        misdirected sentiment,
        gawking onlookers,
        unnecessary grief.
Another lavish waste of time and money,
Perpetuating absurd social custom,
Signifying nothing but idolatry of the transient.

My son. . .
Direct your attention to the soul set free,
        the continuing life,
        the communion of saints.

For it is here,
And not in decaying flesh,
That grief is transformed into joy.

"For what shall it profit a man, if he shall gain the whole world, and lose his own soul?"

Mark 8:36

Insurance

Premiums paid,
Covered for every contingency. . .
Life,
  Health,
    Auto,
      Malpractice,
       Liability,
         Endowment,
          Fire,
           Theft,
            Disability,
Security secured.
Or is it?

Ask yourself, my son. . .
What have you done to insure the immortality of your soul?

"Jesus Christ the same yesterday, and to day, and for ever."

Hebrews 13:8

Missing The Point

Profound thinkers,
Creating movements instead of converts. . .
Theology gone mad.
God an ever changing fad,
Chased after by seekers of the moment,
As if somehow the Gospel changed,
With the writing of every new book.
Surely, Lord,
You must be amused,
If not disgusted.
We, your faithful, always searching. . .
Enchanted by theories,
But ignoring the stability of immutable Scripture.

"For the Holy Ghost shall teach you in the same hour what ye ought to say."

Luke 12:12

A View From The Pulpit

Here before me, Lord,
A reverently disguised sea of faces. . .
Masking a mixture of the critical,
                                receptive,
                                apathetic,
                                disinterested.
Sinners and saints in random array,
Each with different needs,
                         desires,
                         emotions,
                         attitudes.
A potential homiletic nightmare, but yet. . .
Adhering to your Word,
And relying on your inspiration,
The barriers to communication will be transcended by your Spirit.

"Let your light so shine before men, that they may see your good works, and glorify your Father which is in heaven."

Matthew 5:16

Lamps

Lamps lighting the world,
Generated eyes piercing the darkness,
        searching the unknown,
        illuminating the mysterious.
Beacons of truth. . .
All shapes,
   sizes,
   colors,
   intensities.
Spectrums of brilliance. . .
Some glaring,
Others shaded,
Each casting its own reflective gaze upon life's landscape.

Lord, make us penetrating beacons of uncreated light,
That our reflective influence may unite the wavelengths of humanity.
Lord, bring us home again by the invisible wires of your love,
Home to our true source of light. . .
That Light in the face of Christ.

"Hear the right, O Lord, attend unto my cry, give ear unto my prayer, that goeth not out of feigned lips."

Psalm 17:1

In The Valley Of Tears

Lord, it's dark!
Once you were the center of my life,
But now. . . you're gone.
Where are you?
I look. . . but I can't find you.
I call. . . but you don't answer.
I cry. . . but I feel you no longer listen.
Why, Lord?
Why this darkness?
Everything is black,
                confused,
                chaotic.
I pray. . . but my petitions vanish as smoke.
For Christ's sake, help me Lord!
Pierce this darkness,
  Drive away my confusion,
    Instill the light of your presence within my unordered and fearful heart.
Lord, you know I believe. . .
Help my unbelief.

"Even so faith, if it hath not works, is dead, being alone."

James 2:17

The Evening News

Here before my electronic window on life,
I traverse the world in a short thirty minutes.
Wars are waged. . .
    And I dwell secure in peace.
Disaster strikes. . .
    And I sit comfortably in my chair.
Famine runs rampant. . .
    And I gorge myself with food.
Disease kills. . .
    And I rest confidently in health.
Mankind cries out. . .
    And I tell jokes with my friends.
It's so easy Lord to be involved, but yet unengaged.
It's so easy Lord to be informed, but yet apathetic.
It's so easy Lord to be outspoken, but yet inactive.
It's so easy Lord to be concerned, but yet pass the buck.
Help me, Lord, to see life through the window of your Holy Spirit.
Make it difficult for me to stand idle.
Help me, Lord, to be electrified by your Love.

"And the King shall answer and say unto
them, Verily I say unto you, Inasmuch as ye
have done it unto one of the least of these my
brethren, ye have done it unto me."

Matthew 25:40

A Troubled Visitor

He knocked.
I didn't answer.
He knocked.
I shouted, "Come In!"
He spoke.
I said I couldn't be bothered.
He left.

Your body, Lord, is broken.
I broke it!

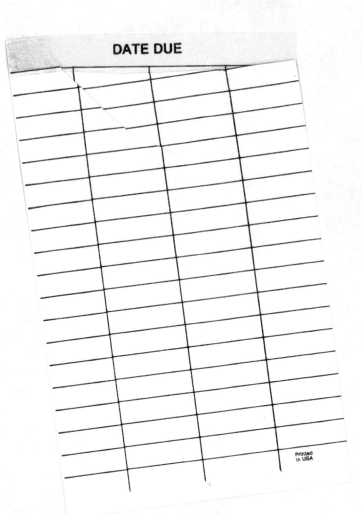

DATE DUE